HEALING FROM A DARK PLACE

MARY HOOKS

www.hisglorycreationspublishing.com

Copyright © 2021 Mary Hooks

All rights reserved. No part of this book may be reproduced in any form without permission in writing from the publisher, except in the case of brief quotations embodied in critical articles or reviews. Unauthorized reproduction of any part of this work is illegal and is punishable by law.

The author and publisher shall have neither liability nor responsibility for anyone with respect to any loss or damage caused directly or indirectly, by the information contained in this book.

ISBN: 978-1-950861-33-0

Scripture references are used with permission from Zondervan via Biblegateway.com

Printed in the United States of America
10 9 8 7 6 5 4 3 2 1

ACKNOWLEDGEMENTS

I would first like to say thank you to my Lord and Savior, Jesus Christ. I give God all the glory for everything he does through this willing vessel.

My motivation; my two wonderful children, Nevaeh Gardner and Alex McDowell Jr., for being so patient and understanding with me as I reach the masses.

Contents

Chapter 1 - Root of Hurt 1

Chapter 2 - Hiding the Hurt 9

Chapter 3 - Airing Out the Wound 13

Chapter 4 - Be Intentional 19

Chapter 5 - Walking It Out 21

CHAPTER 1
Root of Hurt

In life, we experience many obstacles and situations that damage us to a degree. No matter what the situation was for you personally, we have all experienced some type of hurt rather it be physical, mental, or even emotional. As you read along through this book, it is my desire that you will learn how to identify those hurts, acknowledge the hurt, and most importantly, heal from the hurt. So, get something you can write on and take notes as you read along. I want you to focus your full attention on the words in this book. Once you realize how to fully heal and overcome the pain of your past, life will be so much smoother for you. You will feel different. You will breathe differently. You will even view life differently. Dive in with me, and let's take our peace, joy, and life back by force. WE are entitled to it; it belongs to us!

There are various types of hurts we experience throughout life. Emotional hurt is anything that hurts your feelings from a non-physical source. It could simply be something that somebody said to you. It could be as a child that you were physically or even sexually abused by a family friend or stranger, and you never forgave that person. You just kept it a secret and try to continue on with life as if it never happened. (which is why you suffer from trust issues). Maybe you grew up in a single-parent household, and your parent was always working which left you to feel alone because they never had time for you (which is why you suffer from abandonment issues). You may have been the mixed kid in school that got teased because you were too light to be black but too dark to be white, so other children picked on you and made fun of your looks; you didn't fit in with either group (which is why you suffer from identity issues). Do you see yourself in any of these scenarios yet? You may have been the person that was very skinny or the one that had a little more meat on your bones, so you were teased (which is why you suffer from insecurity issues). What about the smart kid with glasses that was always found somewhere reading a book and doing your schoolwork, so you were picked on and called a nerd/ teacher's pet? Or could it be you don't know how to tell people no when you really don't want to do something (which is why you suffer from people-pleasing issues). Being humiliated from the mistakes you have made in the past? Or was it that you were so in love with someone that cheated on you and treated you bad, but you refused to leave and kept giving them chance after chance hoping they would change (which is why you suffer from trust issues). Maybe it's that situation that you got yourself involved in with that married man that you grew a strong intimate bond with and finally had to come to your senses that it could never go any further because he had a wife and children at home (which is why you suffer from low self-esteem issues). Still can't find yourself in any of these scenarios? What about having to bury a child that you carried in your womb and grew to love or a loved one that passed away, and you just couldn't understand how God could allow something like this to happen, so you question God (which is why you suffer from belief issues). I could go on and on because, throughout human life, we experience things that hurt us, but what do we do about that hurt? I really want you to ponder on that question: what do you do about that hurt?

We also may go through a season of our life where we experience a form of physical hurt. Physical hurt is pain in the body; something that causes harm to you through your senses as opposed to your mind. It could include being in a domestic violence situationship/relationship. For some reason, I have been in numerous domestic violence situations, from my ex-pimp to my child's father, and even just men I dated in the past. Yeah, you may be wanting to ask me why do I keep attracting men that want to put their hands on me? Good question. I always wondered that until I stepped back and did a self-evaluation, coming to the conclusion that it was something on the inside of me that felt overlooked and unloved. So, I would attach myself to anything that would give me a little bit of attention and fill that void, which is how I ended up many times with the hands of a man around my neck, being stomped in my head repeatedly, and even a fist hitting me, blackening my eyes.

Or a disease/sickness that has set up camp in your body. At just 26 years old, I was having some digestive issues, so my doctor recommended I see a gastroenterologist. I made an appointment and was examined by the specialist. After the examination, the doctor told me I had an ulcer in my colon and that I would be put on medicine for three weeks; of course, following up with them as well as my primary physician after that three weeks was over. This ulcer brought pain to my body but being a single mother of two children ages 10 and 6, I had to push through the pain and continue to work to provide for my babies: as well as be the chef, the homemaker, and now with the shift in the world, their teacher too. This was a pain/hurt I now had to endure. I knew God to be a healer. His word tells us so in *Isaiah 52:5 But he was wounded for our transgressions, he was bruised for our iniquities: the chastisement of our peace was upon him; and with his stripes we are healed.* Although I couldn't wrap my head around a saved woman of God (not perfect) but determined to live a holy life for Christ now being afflicted in my body. Let me not forget to give you this nugget no matter how saved you are and sold out for Jesus, the enemy is going to try you. Thoughts of doubt came to my mind, even thoughts of fear, but in that very moment, I had to tell the devil he is a liar and he is already defeated. I constantly gave God his word back, altering every ounce of doubt the enemy was trying to plant. With two small children depending on me for their every need, I had no choice but to stand firm on God's word and declare my healing. Physical healing and emotional healing is already ours. That's why it is so important to read the word of God daily and build our faith, knowing that if God is for us, who can be against us.

Mental hurt/ trauma is one we often overlook. We get so used to it. We think this is just how life is, or that's just that person's personality, so we adapt to their trauma, which causes us trauma in another form. Repeated and prolonged exposure to highly stressful events in life is called chronic trauma. This may look like child abuse, domestic violence, a child that has to experience a father in and out of prison. I'm no stranger to chronic trauma. Actually, if I can be transparent with you all, I'm experiencing it now as I write this book. My son's father has been in and out of jail and prison since he was one year's old, and it affects my family in a major way. My son, now six going on seven years old, is trying to cope with the fact that he will miss time with his dad once again; he lashes out, he is angry and upset because he is hurting and can't do anything to get his dad out of prison. As a mom, it hurts to see my child have to bear with such pain at a very young age. Of course, I love him the best way a mother knows how and continues to feed his spirit with the word of God so that he will take a different path. On the other hand, my daughter has become so accustomed to him being incarcerated; when I ask her how she feels about it, her answer is, "it's sad, but daddy always goes to jail, so I'm used to this." Although the children have different views on the situation, it affects them both. It can also cause them to think this is just the way life is, incarceration is normal/ no big deal, or who knows whatever else. This is an example of one person's decisions being detrimental to the next generation.

Acute trauma/ hurt is a one- time dangerous or stressful incident that happens in our life. That could be a car accident, being a victim of a crime, or words that someone spoke to you that really pierced your heart; made you ponder on it even years later, still trying to make sense of it. I remember when I was 15 years old, pregnant with my first child, and hearing my mother telling me to get an abortion because I would never finish high school if I kept my baby. No, I didn't get the abortion. My daughter is now ten years old, healthy, and such a blessing to my life. But it was not until about two years ago that I actually forgave her for what she said. I felt bad enough that I had gotten pregnant at just 15 years old, and for my mother, the person that is supposed to always be there for me supporting and encouraging me, basically says because of my mistake, I would not succeed or be anything was a big slap in the face. Honestly, it left me questioning myself a lot, wondering if I was worthy of better.

Then we have complex trauma. I would say that sums up the year of 2020. Complex trauma is from multiple traumatic events. The COVID-19 world crisis that has caused 406,000 deaths in the United States and still counting; many Americans losing their jobs, homes, vehicles, businesses, and whatever else due to a lack in finances, and all the civil unrest around the United States. Schools/ churches closing, everyone wearing a mask, having to stay 6 ft away from anyone that doesn't live in your home, lockdowns, the list goes on and on. Going unresolved, it has left alot of people seeking therapy, turning to God, and even giving up.

CHAPTER 2
Hiding the Hurt

Do you smoke, drink, close yourself out from the world, or feel depressed? Are you having anxiety attacks, crying yourself to sleep at night, or overthinking? You may be experiencing loss of appetite, a spike in your blood pressure, or PTSD. I know you walk around with a fake smile and act like you are strong and everything is okay, but inside you are balled up in a fetal position screaming to the top of your lungs. Past trauma is an example of how we deal with people in our lives. Experiences mold us into a hard image. The enemy will make us think that acting nonchalantly means you are healed but being non-chalant is not the equivalent of being healed; it is the equivalent to something that you have dealt with for so long you have become numb to that very thing. When we experience hurt, we oftentimes try to ignore the hurt and "move on with life"; I call that the band-aid synopsis.

The band-aid synopsis is where we have a wound(hurt), and instead of dealing with it that very moment, we put a band-aid on it. The band-aid is the addiction we pick up trying to drink, smoke, or even sex the pain away. The band-aid is when we try to suppress the hurt; if someone calls us out of our name, we will say, oh, they are just hating, or we say that's small stuff to a giant. However, in reality it cut you deep, but you refuse to express it, so you use catchy slogans to try and lessen the hurt it left you feeling. You know how we say we don't care to alter the wound we are experiencing. We throw excuses and addictions on top of the wound. Have you ever found yourself being bitter and angry for no reason? It seems like you just snap off about the littlest things. People never know if you are going to be happy or upset because, deep down, you are frustrated and easily irritated. The pain/ hurt has now caused your heart to become hardened. You walk around saying things like I don't trust anybody, so you block out everybody, even those that were really on your side. Now you have built up a wall as tall as the Empire State Building, trying to protect yourself from being hurt again, not realizing that it is the same wall that is keeping you from your healing and blocking out your blessings. Others around you notice the change in your behavior and attitude and tell you that it's something different about you. You are not acting like yourself anymore, throwing a band-aid on top of this wound, unaware that every time we do that, it makes it worse. So just imagine a sore on your hand with all these band-aids piled up on top of it. At this point, it's a nasty wound. It even has a funny stench to it, and it's moist because you wash your hands and shower daily with bandages, but it's not getting any air. As we know, in nature, a sore needs air to heal, and that same thing applies for our emotions. So, we also have to give it air. In this case, God is the air that can and will dry up and heal the wound(hurt). Invite him in as the Ultimate healer he is and allow him to do his best work.

CHAPTER 3

Airing Out the Wound

Now, this part takes some work. This is the part when you make a conscious decision that you want to live better and be better. This is where you are sick and tired of being sick and tired and ready to get over whatever your "it" maybe.

From a spiritual perspective, we are on a journey to wholeness; wholeness demands that we heal. How do we heal? I'm glad you asked! You first have to acknowledge that there are things in your life that hurt you deeply. Once you open up yourself and look back on things and honestly say this thing that so and so said or did hurt, you are on your way to a better place spiritually and emotionally. The enemy loves to keep our mouth shut and our mind wondering, but if you open up your mouth and speak on those things that hurt you, you are already defeating those things that once defeated you. Call those things out into the atmosphere so you can really be healed.

While doing so, your lips may shake, your heart may even begin to beat faster, but do it anyhow with your body trembling, open up your mouth! There is power in your tongue. Break that thing off of your life at the root.

A lot of people will not tell you this, not even pastors, but today I'm going to set somebody free. You can go to church all you want, shout, and even cry and still leave the same. The enemy is not afraid of a church goer, but he does fear someone that is free and has a relationship with Jesus Christ. See, people will attend church just to say I go to church and appear to look righteous but what good is that if you leave bound? Sunday after Sunday; Wednesday after Wednesday; the same cycle carrying the same trauma in and out of church. Honestly, the church benefits from a lot of us being bound; we come in, get a temporary high, pay our tithes and do it all over again week after week. No true freedom; no true transformation. This is where your relationship with Christ comes in. Your personal relationship with the father; the conversations you have with him at your home in the kitchen when nobody else is around. The time you spend laid out in his presence as you feel the comfort and peace knowing he is with you. The tears you cry that only he can interpret when your mouth doesn't have the words to say. You must make yourself vulnerable to God so you can be healed. In God's presence, you do not have to be strong. You do not have to pretend. Tell God what and where it hurts. Generation after generation of abuse, trauma, and hurt. Being molested by caregivers and family members, parents that abandoned us. The parents that didn't know how to speak life over us, the brokenness of soul ties, the secret abortions, the sexual encounters. Confess what has been done to you so you can be free.

STEPS TO HEALING

1. Acknowledge there is a hurt/pain.
2. Be intentional
3. Walking it out

Acknowledge there is hurt/pain: If you are serious about healing and I believe you are if you've made it up to this point in the book; I want you to pray this prayer out loud: Lord God, I come to you broken. I come to you today acknowledging that some things I have been through in my life hurt me; some people hurt me (begin to call out those hurts/people by name). It made me feel like (tell God how it made you feel open up and pour out your heart to him). Lord, I need you to come in and heal the pain that I'm feeling, heal the hurt I still carry from that experience. Father, I come to you, inviting you in to heal me from all my past hurts, pain, and trauma. Every emotional place be healed, every physical place be healed. Every mental place be healed. Create in me a clean heart God so that I can love the people that talked about me, so I can love the people that lied to me, so I can love the people that betrayed me, so I can love the people that used and abused me. I forgive them. Help me Lord, to love your people like you love me when I disappoint you. I believe that my healing is taking place now because you are the ultimate healer, and your word lets me know that healing belongs to me. Now I thank you, Father, and I receive my healing in Jesus's name I pray. Amen.

Saying this prayer is important because we must not only acknowledge our hurt/pain, but we also have to invite the holy spirit in. God is the perfect gentleman. He doesn't just barge his way in. You have to welcome him into those places.

CHAPTER 4

Be Intentional

This part is very vital. During this part of the process, you may have to step away from some people, places, and even things. But when you step away, don't wallow in the pain like a pig in the mud, but do the necessary work to get control over your thoughts. There is a constant battle in the mind. Just like God gives us thoughts of peace, the enemy gives us thoughts of confusion, and we will begin to replay the situation over and over again. The enemy is so sneaky and deceiving. He will have us adding things to it that are not even true—trying to keep us in a bound place. Why be bound when the Lord has given us freedom? Choose freedom and when those thoughts of the situation come up, speak out of your mouth and say what God says. Declare that you are not in that place anymore and that you are already free from that place. Once you make a habit of rejecting those thoughts that don't agree with what the word of the Lord says, they will stop. The bible tells us in *James 4:7 Therefore submit to God. Resist the devil and he will flee from you. (NKJV)* Keep applying the word of God, and you will overcome anything that comes your way. Now, remember this is no magic trick. You will have ups and downs during the process of healing. Some days you are going to feel like you are on the mountain top. And some days, you are going to feel like you are in the valley. Although the valley may not feel good, it's needed as well. On the valley days, let the emotions flow and cry if you need to. This is a part of the process. We are humans, and we are emotional creatures. We are designed to feel. It's absolutely normal. Don't quench the emotions. There is a cleansing taking place when we release tears.

CHAPTER 5

Walking It Out

God is always doing something new. He is always moving and shifting things to elevate and go higher. This reminds me of a scripture in the bible *Matthew 9:16-17 No one sews a patch of unshrunk cloth on an old garment, for the patch will pull away from the garment, making the tear worse. Neither do people pour new wine into old wineskins. If they do, the skins will brust; the wine will run out and the wineskins will be ruined. No, they pour new wine into new wineskins, and both are preserved.* We cannot experience the new things that God is trying to do in our lives if we hold on to the things of the past. God has so much more in store for us if we can just accept the past for what it was and let go of those experiences. Old mindsets(wineskins) will burst if we don't release them. If we truly want to receive the newness of life, the newness of joy, the newness of peace, the newness of love, we must open ourselves up to a new mindset(wineskins), that way we may be filled by the new revelation of what God is doing in our life. But first, we

must forget those things that are behind us *Isaiah 43:18-19*
Forget the former things; do not dwell on the past. See, I am doing a new thing! Now it springs up; do you not perceive it? I am making a way in the wilderness and streams in the wasteland.

HEALING SCRIPTURES

Psalm 147:3 He heals the brokenhearted and binds up their wounds.

Psalm 30:2 Lord my God, I called to you for help, and you healed me.

Matthew 11:28 "Come to me, all you who are weary and burdened, and I will give you rest.

Jeremiah 30:17 But I will restore you to health and heal your wounds, declares the Lord

Isaiah 33:2 Lord, be gracious to us; we long for you. Be our strength every morning, our salvation in time of distress.

Revelation 21:4 And God will wipe every tear from their eyes. There will be no more death or mourning or crying or pain, for the former things have passed away.

Psalm 73:26 My flesh and my heart may fail, but God is the strength of my heart and my portion forever.

John 14:27 Peace I leave with you; my peace I give you. I do not give to you as the world gives. Do not let your hearts be troubled and do not be afraid.

James 5:16 Therefore confess your sins to each other and pray for each other so that you may be healed. The prayer of the righteous person is powerful and effective.

Luke 6:19 and the people all tried to touch him, because power was coming from him and healing them all.

Matthew 9:35 Jesus went through all the towns and villages, teaching in their synagogues, proclaiming the good news of the kingdom and healing every disease and sickness.

Psalm 23:1-4 The Lord is my shepherd, I lack nothing. He makes me lie down in green pastures, he leads me beside quiet waters, he refreshes my soul. He guides me along the right paths for his name sake. Even though I walk through the darkest valley, I will fear no evil, for you are with me; your rod and your staff, they comfort me.

Proverbs 3:5-8 Trust in the Lord with all your heart and lean not to your own understanding; in all your ways submit to him, and he will make your paths straight. Do not be in your own eyes; fear the Lord and shun evil. This will bring health to your body and nourishment to your bones.

Jeremiah 17:14 Heal me, Lord, and I will be healed; save me and I will be saved, for you are the one I praise.

Psalm 6:2 Have mercy on me, Lord, for I am faint; heal me, Lord, for my bones are in agony.

Exodus 23: 25-26 Worship the Lord your God, and his blessing will be on your food and water. I will take away sickness from among you, and none will miscarry or be barren in your land. I will give you a full life span.

Now I could not close this book out without offering salvation. I don't know who you are or the path that you have walked. But I do know that Jesus loves you. I do know that he died on the cross for you, and if you want to be saved, he is waiting for you with open arms.

We all get to a point in life where we are tired of trying to do things our way. If you are at that point in your life, I want to allow you the opportunity to give your life to Christ today.

The Prayer of Salvation: Lord God, I ask that you forgive me for I have sinned. I come to you asking that you wash me clean and renew my mind. I believe your son Jesus Christ died on the cross and rose from the dead. I invite you into my heart and my life. I accept you as my Lord and Savior. This day I choose to follow you, and I decree that I am saved in the name of Jesus, Amen.

Healing looks good on you! Freedom and deliverance is your portion. Go forth and do not turn around. There is absolutely nothing back there for you.

MY HEALING JOURNAL

MY HEALING JOURNAL

MY HEALING JOURNAL

MY HEALING JOURNAL

MY HEALING JOURNAL

MY HEALING JOURNAL

MY HEALING JOURNAL

MY HEALING JOURNAL

MY HEALING JOURNAL

MY HEALING JOURNAL

About the Author

Mary Hooks, a mother of two children, grew up in Milwaukee, Wisconsin, where the street life tried to take her out. She was a teen mom involved in prostitution, drug/alcoholism, and domestic violence. What the enemy meant for evil, God turned for good.

As a businesswoman, Mary is the COO of sheOVERCOMER, LLC., because God is the CEO. sheOVERCOMER,LLC is a brand that represents the woman that has overcome the many obstacles life has thrown at her. It is her mission to help young girls and women that are battling with the same issues she has endured as well as preventing others from falling into such a dark lifestyle.

Mary is also the author of "Be Completely Comfortable with the Unique Way God Made You" and a Co-Author in Down for The Count, Volume Two: Bouncing Back from Life's Blows.

Email: hooksmary49@gmail.com
Website: www.sheovercomer.com
Instagram: maryhooks18

His Glory Creations Publishing, LLC is an International Christian Book Publishing Company, which helps launch the creative works of new, aspiring and seasoned authors across the globe, through stories that are inspirational, empowering, life-changing or educational in nature, including poetry, journals, children's books, fiction and non-fiction works.

DESIRE TO KNOW MORE ABOUT HGCP?

Contact Information:
CEO/Founder: Felicia C. Lucas
www.hisglorycreationspublishing.com
Facebook: His Glory Creations Publishing
Email: hgcpublishingllc@gmail.com
Phone: 919-679-1706

www.ingramcontent.com/pod-product-compliance
Lightning Source LLC
Chambersburg PA
CBHW052127110526
44592CB00013B/1789